Prentice Hall

LITERATURE
Timeless Voices, Timeless Themes

Standardized Test Preparation Answers and Explanations on Transparencies

BRONZE

D1311321

PRENTICE HALL
Upper Saddle River, New Jersey
Glenview, Illinois
Needham, Massachusetts

ISBN 0-13-0508101

1 2 3 4 5 6 7 8 9 10   03 02 01 00 99

Table of Contents

Table of Contents (continued)

Use Context Clues (p. 1)

1	A	4	C
2	D	5	D
3	B	6	C

Use Context Clues (p. 2)

1	D	4	B
2	C	5	A
3	B	6	D

Use Context Clues (p. 3)

1	A	4	D
2	B	5	C
3	A	6	D

Use Context Clues (p. 4)

1	B	4	A
2	A	5	A
3	D	6	B

Use Context Clues (p. 5)

1	C	4	C
2	A	5	D
3	A	6	A

Use Context Clues (p. 6)

1	A	4	C
2	D	5	D
3	C	6	B

Use Context Clues (p. 7)

1	B	4	B
2	D	5	C
3	A	6	D

Use Context Clues (p. 8)

1	A	4	D
2	D	5	B
3	C	6	B

Use Context Clues (p. 9)

1	A	4	A
2	B	5	C
3	D		

Arrange Events In Sequential Order (p. 10)

1	C	4	A
2	B	5	D
3	B		

Arrange Events In Sequential Order (p. 11)

1	C	4	A
2	D	5	D
3	C	6	B

Arrange Events In Sequential Order (p. 12)

1	D	4	A
2	D	5	B
3	C	6	A

Arrange Events In Sequential Order (p. 13)

1	D	4	D
2	C	5	C
3	B	6	C

Arrange Events In Sequential Order (p. 14)

1	B	3	D
2	A	4	A

Arrange Events In Sequential Order (p. 15)

1	D	3	A
2	C	4	B

Identify Main Idea (p. 16)

1	B	4	C
2	A	5	B
3	D		

Identify Main Idea (p. 17)

1	D	3	B
2	B	4	A

Identify Main Idea (p. 18)

1	A	3	B
2	C	4	D

Identify Main Idea (p. 19)

1	D	4	A
2	D	5	C
3	B		

Identify Main Idea (p. 20)

1	C	3	A
2	D	4	B

Identify Main Idea (p. 21)

1	A	4	A
2	D	5	C
3	C		

Recognize Point of View (p. 22)

1	C	4	C
2	D	5	C
3	A	6	B

Recognize Point of View (p. 23)

1	B	4	A
2	B	5	C
3	D		

Recognize Point of View (p. 24)

1 C
2 D
3 A
4 A
5 D
6 B

Recognize Point of View (p. 25)

1 A
2 D
3 D
4 B
5 C

Recognize Point of View (p. 26)

1 D
2 A
3 A
4 B
5 C
6 C

Recognize Point of View (p. 27)

1 B
2 A
3 B
4 A
5 D

Draw Inferences; Generalizations (p. 28)

1 C
2 B
3 D
4 A

Draw Inferences; Generalizations (p. 29)

1 B
2 A
3 A
4 D

Draw Inferences; Generalizations (p. 30)

1 D
2 C
3 C
4 C

Draw Inferences; Generalizations (p. 31)

1 C
2 C
3 D
4 B

Draw Inferences; Generalizations (p. 32)

1 B
2 D
3 A
4 C

Draw Inferences; Generalizations (p. 33)

1 D
2 A
3 B
4 A

Predict Outcomes (p. 34)

1 D
2 C
3 A
4 B

Predict Outcomes (p. 35)

1 A
2 C
3 D
4 C

Predict Outcomes (p. 36)

1 C
2 A
3 D
4 C

Predict Outcomes (p. 37)

1 B
2 C
3 A
4 D

Predict Outcomes (p. 38)

1 B
2 C
3 D
4 C

Predict Outcomes (p. 39)

1 A
2 C
3 D
4 D

Distinguish Fact and Opinion (p. 40)

1 B
2 A
3 D
4 A

Recognize the Author's Purpose (p. 41)

1 C
2 B
3 D
4 C
5 D

Fact and Opinion (p. 42)

1 A
2 A
3 B
4 C

Author's Point of View (p. 43)

1 D
2 C
3 A
4 B
5 C

Recognize Author's Purpose and Main Idea (p. 44)

1 B
2 D
3 C
4 D

Recognize Appropriate Usage (p. 45)

1 C
2 D
3 A

Recognize Appropriate Usage (p. 46)

1 A
2 C
3 D

Recognize Appropriate Usage (p. 47)

1 A
2 C
3 A

Recognize Appropriate Usage (p. 48)

1 C
2 B
3 C

Recognize Appropriate Usage (p. 49)

1 B
2 C
3 A
4 C
5 D
6 C

Appropriate Usage (p. 50)

1 B
2 A
3 D
4 D
5 B
6 C

Appropriate Usage (p. 51)

1	B	4	B
2	C	5	D
3	A	6	C

Appropriate Usage (p. 52)

1	C	4	B
2	A	5	B
3	D	6	C

Appropriate Usage (p. 53)

1	A	4	D
2	C	5	B
3	D	6	C

Appropriate Usage (p. 54)

1	B	4	D
2	C	5	C
3	D	6	D

Appropriate Usage (p. 55)

1	D	4	A
2	B	5	A
3	D	6	B

Appropriate Usage (p. 56)

1	A	4	C
2	B	5	A
3	D	6	B

Recognize Appropriate Spelling, Capitalization, and Punctuation (p. 57)

1	C	4	A
2	B	5	D
3	B	6	C

Recognize Appropriate Spelling, Capitalization, and Punctuation (p. 58)

1	B	4	A
2	A	5	C
3	B	6	D

Recognize Appropriate Spelling, Capitalization, and Punctuation (p. 59)

1	B	4	D
2	C	5	A
3	D	6	A

Recognize Appropriate Spelling, Capitalization, and Punctuation (p. 60)

1	C	4	D
2	B	5	A
3	C	6	C

Recognize Appropriate Spelling, Capitalization, and Punctuation (p. 61)

1	B	4	C
2	B	5	C
3	A	6	D